LIFT-THE-FLAP
BIBLE STORIES

Christina Goodings
Illustrated by Annabel Hudson

LION
CHILDREN'S

creation

In the beginning, God made the world.
God made the sky above the land.
God made the sea around the land.

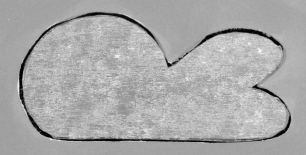

God made the birds that fly in the sky.
God made the fish that swim in the sea.

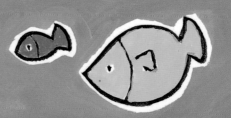

Noah

God told Noah to build an ark.
When the flood came, Noah and his family
were safe inside with all the animals.

When the flood was
over, God put a rainbow
in the sky.

Baby Moses

'Oh dear,' said the mother. 'The king's soldiers
are coming to take all baby boys away.
'I won't let them find my baby.
'I shall hide him.'

Then she and little Miriam went
down to the river.
They hid the cradle in the reeds.

The princess came to
the river to bathe.
'What's in that
basket?' she said.

Brave David

King Saul frowned.
His soldiers frowned too.
'Here comes the enemy,' they said.
'Who will fight them?' asked the king.

'Ha! Ha! Ha!' laughed Goliath.
'Don't you know who I am?'
'I do,' said David. 'I believe God
will help me beat you!'

David went to fight.
He slung a stone
at the giant.

Jonah and the Whale

There was a storm at sea.
'It's all my fault,' said Jonah.
'I disobeyed God.'
So Jonah went into the sea.

The whale took Jonah to land.
'I shall obey God,' said Jonah.
'I shall go to Nineveh.'

'Listen,' he told the people there.
'Obey God or there will be trouble.'
'We will,' they said.
And everyone was happy.

Daniel and the Lions

Daniel was in trouble. He was being
punished for saying his prayers.
He was being thrown to the lions.

God did not want Daniel to be hurt,
so God sent an angel.

Baby Jesus

Here are Mary and Joseph.
Baby Jesus is cradled in the manger.
Who has come to see him?

The Two Builders

When Jesus grew up, he told this story:
'One man built his house high on a rock.
'The rain came.
'The wind blew.

'The house was safe above the flood.'

'Do the good things I say,' said Jesus,
'or you will be like the person who built
his house on sand.
'The rain came.
'The wind blew.

The Lost Sheep

Jesus told a story:

'There was once a shepherd who had a hundred sheep.

'But one was fond of mischief. It ran away.

'The shepherd went looking.

'He looked everywhere.
'He was very worried.

Zacchaeus

Zacchaeus was short.
He was also a cheat.
'But I want to see Jesus,'
whimpered Zacchaeus.
'I know what to do.'

Jesus knew where he was.
'Come down out of that tree,' he called.
'I want to stay at your house today.'

Zacchaeus took Jesus to his house. He listened to what Jesus had to say. Then he said something surprising. 'I'm not going to be a cheat any more. I want to be friends with everyone.'

The First Easter

When Jesus died on a cross, his friends laid him in a tomb.
But when they went to say a last goodbye, the tomb was empty.
'What has happened?' they asked.